DATE DUE

DATE DUE			
NOV 26			
JUN 28			
OCT 26			
NOV 22			
JUL 13			
MAR 14			
FEB 24			
JUN 28			
MAY 27			
APR 17 2001			
FEB 19 2002			
402			
104			
405			
GAYLORD			PRINTED IN U.S.A

Events of the Revolution

Battle for Quebec,

by Susan and John Lee

Illustrated by Robert Ulm

 CHILDRENS PRESS, CHICAGO

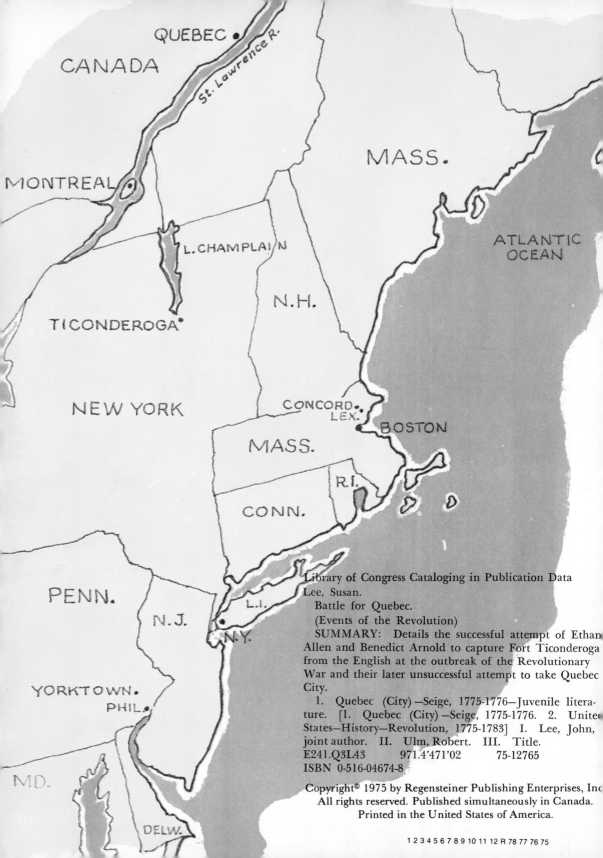

QUEBEC .

CANADA

St. Lawrence R.

MONTREAL

MASS.

L.CHAMPLAIN

ATLANTIC
OCEAN

N.H.

TICONDEROGA.

NEW YORK

CONCORD..
LEX.

BOSTON

MASS.

R.I.

CONN.

PENN.

L.I.

N.J.

N.Y.

YORKTOWN.

PHIL.

MD.

DELW.

Library of Congress Cataloging in Publication Data

Lee, Susan.

Battle for Quebec.

(Events of the Revolution)

SUMMARY: Details the successful attempt of Ethan Allen and Benedict Arnold to capture Fort Ticonderoga from the English at the outbreak of the Revolutionary War and their later unsuccessful attempt to take Quebec City.

1. Quebec (City) —Seige, 1775-1776—Juvenile literature. [1. Quebec (City) —Seige, 1775-1776. 2. United States—History—Revolution, 1775-1783] I. Lee, John, joint author. II. Ulm, Robert. III. Title.

E241.Q3L43   971.4'471'02   75-12765

ISBN 0-516-04674-8

1 2 3 4 5 6 7 8 9 10 11 12 R 78 77 76 75

Before Quebec, 1775

At Lexington, the English fired and Americans fell dead. At Concord, the English fired again but the Americans fired back. From Concord back to Boston, men died on both sides. The English pulled back into Boston.

Down from New Hampshire came John Stark and his fighting men. An old Ranger, Israel Putman, led 3,000 men up from Connecticut. From Rhode Island marched men headed by tall, limping Nathanael Greene. This American army surrounded Boston.

Up in the New Hampshire Grants (now Vermont), Ethan Allen got ready to fight. He wasn't going to Boston. His Green Mountain Boys were going to fight closer to home.

Chapter 1
THE GREEN MOUNTAIN BOYS

Will Campbell sat in a Farmington tavern. Around him were all the important people in town. For the first time in his life, everyone was waiting for Will to talk.

"Come on, Will," said the tavern owner. "Tell us how you beat the English. Tell us how you captured Fort Ticonderoga."

"Yes sir," said young Will Campbell. "You all know Ethan Allen. Born in Connecticut. Went up to the Green Mountain country. He's a big, rough man. Some say he could fight a bear with his hands and win."

"We know about Allen," someone said. "Tell us about the fighting at the fort."

"Well, Allen's head of the Green Mountain Boys. They are tough mountain men. All Indian fighters. They stay alive by being good with a musket and a knife. Allen's their colonel. He's not a real colonel, of course. They just say he's one. And nobody else dares say he isn't. Nobody argues with those Green Mountain Boys."

"We know about the Green Mountain Boys," said the tavern owner. "And we know that Connecticut money pays for their gunpowder. We're the ones who gave Allen the idea of capturing the fort. Now, *please,* tell us about the fighting."

"Colonel Allen sent word for his men to join him in Bennington. They were to come ready to fight the English. I was working on a farm nearby. I went in to see what was up. The Green Mountain Boys came in. They'd follow

Allen anywhere. I got so worked up I went along."

"How old are you?" asked someone.

"I'm 19 and I had my own gun and powder. Allen had about 230 of us. We marched out of Bennington. We took the road up the east side of the river. Up north, we cut over to the road close to Lake George."

"We got to Lake George on May 9th. We could look across and see the fort. The colonel sent us out to look for boats, canoes, anything. We were afraid the colonel might make us swim if we didn't find boats."

Everyone laughed. Someone filled Will's mug.

"We found some boats. Not many, but some. Some of us rowed across the lake. Colonel Allen sent the boats back for more men. Colonel Seth Warner led the men on the east shore.

"It began to get light. The sun wasn't up, but we could see each other. There were 83 of us on the west shore. Then Colonel Allen said he wasn't going to wait for the others. He said he was going up to the fort.

"He said we didn't have to go with him. He said only brave men could march with him. If anyone wanted to stay back, that was all right with him. No one was about to stay behind. We got into three lines. Allen got in front of the middle line. Then we marched to old Fort Ticonderoga.

"There was one English sentry at the gate. The colonel ran at the sentry. The sentry ran inside the fort. We ran inside. There was a parade ground with barracks on two sides. Half of us lined up facing the east barracks. Half of us faced the west barracks. Two English sentries walked up to us. One of them stuck the tip of his bayonet in one of our men. Didn't hurt him much.

"Colonel Allen whacked the sentry with the side of his sword. Both sentries dropped their muskets. Allen asked where their leader was.

The sentry said Captain de la Place was their leader. He said his room was on the second floor of the west barracks.

"Colonel Allen ran up the stairs. He banged on the door. Captain Place came out rubbing his eyes with one hand. He held his pants in his other hand. Colonel Allen told him to surrender the fort.

"Captain Place asked in whose name he was to surrender. 'In the name of the great Jehovah, and the Continental Congress,' yells the colonel.

"We knocked down the barracks doors and took about 50 English prisoners. We also got about 100 cannon. About then the sun came out shining nice and bright. So we sat down and ate English food for breakfast."

"No one got killed?" someone asked. "You mean you took the fort without shooting?"

"It wasn't no trouble at all," said Will Campbell. "Then Colonel Warner came marching up with the rest of the men. He was mad because he'd missed all the fun. Colonel Allen said if he wanted some fun to go capture Crown Point up the river."

Someone poured another mug of rum for Will.

"So Colonel Warner took 100 men and captured Crown Point. There were only 13 or 14 English soldiers there. But there were another

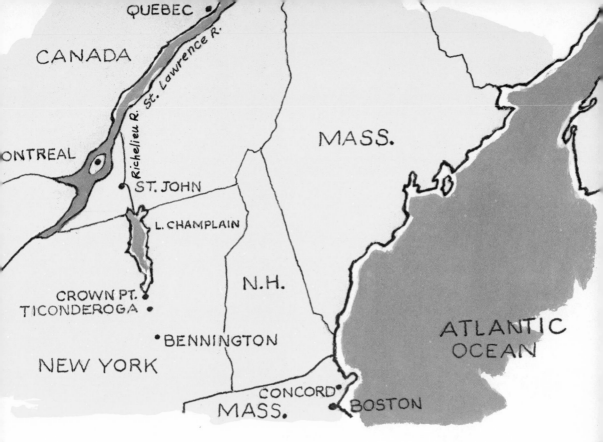

100 cannon in that old fort. That made Warner happy.

"Later, Colonel Allen heard there was an old English ship at St. John. We found one at South Bay on Lake Champlain. Benedict Arnold said he knew how to sail. So we put some men and small cannon on that ship. Arnold said he was a colonel from Massachusetts, but Ethan Allen called him a captain. They didn't get along too well. Benedict Arnold wants to run everything. Arnold's smart and he's brave; but no one runs Ethan Allen.

"Anyway, Allen let Arnold sail the ship. He was to sail north on Lake Champlain. Then north up the Richelieu River to St. John. The rest of us were to row the boats behind him. The wind came up out of the south. Arnold's ship sailed out of sight.

"We were still rowing up the lake when Captain Arnold comes back. But now he's got two ships. He'd captured St. John and the English ship and sailed back."

Will put down his mug and said, "That's the true story of how we captured three forts between here and Canada."

Chapter 2
MONTGOMERY'S MUSKETS

Will left the tavern and walked to his mother's farm. Over supper, he told his story again to his younger brothers. They were excited by the idea of fighting in a war.

"You are all after blood," said Will. "But what if you are the one who is shot? War is easy only in a story."

"But we are winning, aren't we?" asked 16-year-old Dick Campbell. "We ran the English out of Concord. We penned them up in Boston. Allen won at Fort Ticonderoga. I want to see some fighting before the war is over."

"Dick," said Will, "we fought like Indians at Concord. We captured Ticonderoga from men who didn't know there was fighting down here. Don't you think the English will win some of the time? Don't be a fool. You stay home and help with the farm."

Will stayed home. He didn't talk more about Ticonderoga. He didn't want Dick joining the army.

In mid-July, Will packed up. He went back to work on the farm outside Bennington. At night the farmers sat in a tavern and talked about Indians. One night a hunter joined the farmers.

"The English give muskets and powder to the Indians," the hunter said. "First thing you know they'll be down here burning your farms. Then they'll move into New York."

"Won't the soldiers at Fort Ticonderoga stop them?" asked a young man.

"No, sonny," said the hunter. "Indians will go around the fort. They'll go after farms and small towns. The English at St. John will give them all the powder they need. The redcoats will help the redskins burn your farms."

"Maybe we should go back to St. John," said Will. "We can capture it again."

"Not without a bigger army, you won't," said the hunter. The English are turning St. John into a fort. It'll be hard to capture it again."

In Philadelphia the Continental Congress was also thinking about Canada. They sent orders to General Schuyler of New York. He was to capture St. John and Montreal. Then, if he wanted, he could try to capture Quebec. If he could take Quebec, the English would have to leave Canada.

In Ticonderoga, the Americans got ready. General Schuyler was not there yet. Richard Montgomery was the leader. Montgomery had been a member of the English Parliament. He also had been an officer in the English army. Now he was an American general.

At sunset on August 28, 1775 General Montgomery led 1,200 soldiers out of Fort Ticonderoga. Most of the soldiers were from New York or Connecticut. Ethan Allen was along with some of his Green Mountain Boys. Will Campbell was with Allen.

The men loaded into ships, boats, and canoes. They headed north on Lake Champlain. On September 3, 1775 they were at the north end of the lake. There, General Schuyler joined them. He had 700 more soldiers with him.

The next day, most of the soldiers began marching along the east bank of the Richelieu

River. There were roads at some places. There were no roads much of the way.

Ethan Allen and Major Brown were sent to visit the Canadian towns. They were to tell the Canadians that the Americans came as friends. They came to fight the English, not the Canadians.

Schuyler's army slopped through swamps. They climbed hills. They walked through heavy rains. General Schuyler became sick. At last the army reached St. John. They found it was now a good fort. Some 600 English soldiers defended the fort.

The Americans attacked. The English drove them off. The Americans attacked again. The English drove them off again. Then General Schuyler got so sick he had to go back to New York.

General Montgomery took over. The Americans didn't know just what to do. Some officers wanted one plan. Others had their own plans. Montgomery had trouble making the Americans work together.

Montgomery sent Allen and a few men back into the woods. Will Campbell was one who went with Allen. Allen went to the town of Sorel. Then he started west along the St. Lawrence River. On September 24, 1775 he left the town of Longueuil. With him were 80 men, mostly Canadians. Then he met Major Brown with his 200 men.

Allen and Brown cooked up a plan to capture Montreal, an island town. Allen was to go back to Longueuil and get some canoes. His men were to land north of Montreal. Brown was to land south of Montreal. Then both would attack on the twenty-fifth and capture Montreal.

Allen picked up 30 more men and the canoes. He crossed the St. Lawrence and camped. Major Brown could not cross the river. In the morning, the English discovered Allen's camp. About 500 English, Canadians, and Indians attacked Allen's men.

The fight didn't last long. Allen and most of his Canadians were captured. Will Campbell got away. He found a canoe and got back to the town of La Prairie. From there he walked through the woods until he got to St. John.

On October 18, Major Brown captured Fort Chambly. It was north of St. John, so the English were trapped. No help could come down the river to them.

After 50 days of fighting, the Americans captured St. John. The 600 English soldiers were prisoners. On November 5, Montgomery set out for Montreal. It was snowing as his soldiers marched.

On November 13, 1775 the Americans captured Montreal. The governor of Canada, General Guy Carleton, got away. He went to defend Quebec.

Not many Canadians joined the Americans. They had seen Allen's little army captured. They wouldn't take sides. They would wait and see what happened.

Will Campbell sat by the St. Lawrence River. "I'm sure glad my brother isn't in this," he said. "He thinks war is a game. Look at us. We're cold, sick, tired. Now we've got to get to Quebec in the winter snow. I'm glad Dick's not in this sort of trouble."

Will was wrong. Dick was in Canada. And his trip to the St. Lawrence had been worse than Will's.

Chapter 3
ARNOLD'S RIFLEMEN

In late August, Dick Campbell heard news of Canada. Another American army was being sent there. This army was to meet at Cambridge in Massachusetts.

Dick went out the attic window. His bare feet hugged the wooden shingles of the porch roof. Move like an Indian, he kept telling himself. If Mom wakes up, I'm in trouble.

An old oak grew by the porch. Dick stepped onto a thick branch. He sat down, swung from the branch, and dropped to the ground. He moved across the yard and into the road. Only then did he put on his shoes. He was on his way to Cambridge.

Inside the house his mother felt the tears on her cheek. "Another son gone," she said. "Let this war end, dear God, before the little ones go too."

Dick cut east to Hartford on the Connecticut River. There he turned north for Springfield. From there he walked the post road to Boston. He made good time in the river valleys. He was young enough to make good time even in the mountains.

Farmers fed him and let him sleep in their barns. They asked where he was going. He told them he was joining Washington. Some of the families were loyal to King George. But even they would feed a hungry boy.

Dick smelled the ocean before he saw it. American soldiers showed him the road to Cambridge. There he found Connecticut troops under Colonel Roger Enos. The soldiers told him what they knew.

"Most of us are from New England," said Caleb Brown. "But there's mountain boys from

Virginia and Pennsylvania. They got rifles and can hit a redcoat at 200 yards. We got muskets that are good for 50, maybe 60 yards. We can load faster than they can, but we sure can't shoot as far."

"Who's our leader?" asked Dick.

"Colonel Benedict Arnold."

"He was with my brother and Ethan Allen at Fort Ticonderoga. Will says he's a wild, brave man."

"Eh yup," said Caleb. "He'll be a wild one to follow. Sure wants his own way. Thinks he's the smartest man in the army."

Dick got a look at the riflemen. They wore brown deerskin shirts. He saw them shooting at little marks. Again and again they hit the marks. Dick began to wish he owned a rifle.

"Who's that?" he asked Caleb.

"Captain Daniel Morgan," said Caleb. "He's top officer of the riflemen."

"He's sure big," said Dick.

"He's got to be big," said Caleb. "Those boys don't like to take orders. They make more trouble than the rest of the army put together. It takes a big man to make them do what he says."

"Who's that one?" Dick asked.

"That's Febiger," said Caleb. "He's from Denmark. He was at Breed's Hill. He runs things for Colonel Arnold."

On September 13, 1775, the 1,100 man army
marched out of Cambridge. They took the road
to Newburyport. There they climbed into
waiting ships. The ships took them to the mouth
of the Kennebec River.

New rowboats lined the banks of the river.
Made of pine, they had flat bottoms for river
travel. The wood was green (newly cut). They
had been built in a hurry. They would leak, but
they would have to do.

The men piled into the boats and started up the river. The weather was good. They ate and slept well. They were moving slowly, but they were on their way. Then things went bad in a hurry.

It began to rain hard. No one could stay dry. They came to rapids in the river. The men waded and pulled the boats through the rapids. Some boats turned over. Some broke up on the rocks. Food and powder were lost.

Things got worse. It went on raining. It got colder every day. More and more food was lost as boats broke up. The men ate their pet dogs. Then they boiled leather and ate it.

They came to a portage (a carrying place between two rivers). They had to cross ten miles of swamps and hills. They had to cut a path so they could carry their boats. The men thought it was funny that they were going to the Dead River.

Nothing else was funny. The men were wet and cold. They were tired and hungry. Many were sick. They reached the Dead River on October 15, 1775.

That night the men ate a soup made from candles. Colonel Enos told Arnold he was taking his men home. Arnold didn't like it, but he couldn't stop them.

Dick went to see Captain Morgan. "I got a brother with Montgomery in Canada. I can't turn back. Can I go on with you?"

Captain Morgan said Dick could join his riflemen. Dick went to shake hands with Caleb. "When you get back, go see my Mom. Tell her I'm fine. Don't tell her how bad things are here."

The army started up the Dead River. Again they had to fight rapids and rocks. It went on raining. More and more men fell sick.

They came to the next portage. It was about 12 miles to the Chaudière River. They had to climb higher hills than before. It began to snow.

The men carried their boats through mud and snow. Some men fell and never got up. They died where they lay. No one was strong enough to bury them.

Dick Campbell was lucky. He had worked hard on the farm. He was young and he was strong. He walked like he was asleep, but he wasn't sick.

The men got to the Chaudière River. This river flowed north into Canada. It was easy to row with the flow of water. Dick had a deerskin shirt and a rifle. He had taken both off a dead rifleman. The men killed a few deer along the river. No one got enough to eat, but it was better than candle soup.

They made one more portage. They marched six miles to the south bank of the St. Lawrence River. On November 9, 1775, they stood on Point Levi and looked across at Quebec. Of the 1,100 men who started, only 600 were left.

Chapter 4
QUEBEC

General Arnold thought his men could capture Quebec. Cold, hungry soldiers would fight to capture food and warm houses. Then it began to storm. The wind was so strong Arnold couldn't get boats across the river.

English ships could move on the river even if boats couldn't. Ships and men came in to help defend Quebec. The storm ended on November 13. By then General Carleton had 1,200 men. Now Colonel Arnold had to wait. His army wasn't strong enough to attack.

Arnold and his soldiers crossed the river west of Quebec. There he met General Montgomery who had marched up from Montreal. Between them, they had about 1,000 men.

Montgomery had captured a warehouse full of English winter uniforms. Now, Arnold's soldiers could at least be warm. Will Campbell was handing out heavy coats to Arnold's men. His head jerked up when he heard someone say, "Hello, brother."

Will looked up to see Dick in front of him. "Dick," he yelled, "how did you get here?"

"Came up the rivers with Arnold," Dick said. The two brothers hugged each other. "I thought you were done with war," said Dick. "How come you're here?"

Will grinned. "I listened to Ethan Allen again. First thing I knew I was walking behind him into Canada. But you! Did you run away from home?"

"Yep," said Dick, "and many a day I wished I was back on the farm. I signed up to fight until December 31. Then I'm going home."

"You do that," said Will. "Don't listen to any sweet talk. Do your duty till your time's up. Then go home. And stay home!"

Soldiers from the two armies sat around and talked. What was Quebec like? Would it be hard to capture? Where would the attack take place?

"Quebec is built on top of a cliff," said Dick.

"That means all the roads run uphill to the town," said Will. "Are there steep cliffs on three sides of the town?"

"Yep," said Dick, "that's the Upper Town. It's partly surrounded by a thirty-foot wall, too. Just below it is the Lower Town. That's where the docks and warehouses are. There are stores with people living above them. You have to climb a steep hill to get from one part of town to the other."

"What about the streets?" asked Will.

"They aren't wide, but they're crooked as can be."

"We are going to have trouble finding our way around in streets like that," said Will. "Maybe we should grow wings and fly into town."

The officers were also making their plans. The Americans had some small cannons. But they weren't big enough to shoot down the gates in the wall. The Americans didn't have enough men to attack the walls. Quebec was really one big fort.

On December 16, 1775, the American officers made their plans. They would attack at night. They would use four groups of men. Two groups would be small. They would make fake attacks at Quebec's gates. Two groups would be large. They would make the real attacks against the Lower Town.

Montgomery's men would come in from the west. They would use the only road between the river and the cliffs. They were to smash into the heart of Lower Town.

Arnold's men were to attack from the east. They were to join up with Montgomery in Lower

Town. Then both groups would climb the steep hill leading into Upper Town.

The officers let their men rest. They fed them all the food they could get. Arnold's men began to gain back the pounds they had lost on their trip. Rifles and muskets were cleaned. Powder was checked to be sure it was dry. The little army was getting ready to fight.

Will was going with Montgomery's men. Dick was still with Morgan's riflemen, so he would follow Arnold. They both waited, and each hoped the other wouldn't be killed.

It started to snow hard on the night of December 30. The wind blew the snow into high drifts. In Quebec, the snow piled up in the streets. No one could see more than a few feet in the dark and snow.

There was a log fence across the road at the west end of Lower Town. Behind it was a blockhouse. Inside the blockhouse were 50 English and Canadian soldiers. They had three cannon pointed at the fence. One was always kept loaded with grapeshot (a handful of musketballs).

In the early hours of December 31, 1775, the Americans began to move. An English soldier watched the road from the blockhouse. Suddenly he blinked his eyes. The snowy road was growing darker. A dark mass was moving toward him.

Then the dark mass stopped. Through the snow came a few men. They were checking the log fence. Now the soldier knew that the dark mass was the American army.

Some men came over the fence. They moved slowly across the snow. The English soldier held a match to the cannon loaded with grapeshot. Red flame shot out its barrel. The grapeshot flew out! The smoke cleared. Every man in front of the fence was down. All were dead or dying.

The English reloaded. The Americans did not attack. They fell back. Soon no one could be seen on the road.

Will Campbell lay behind the log fence. A grapeshot had hit him in the arm. He didn't feel any pain. His arm felt like it was made of ice. He looked at his hand. Blood was running off the tips of his fingers.

Will peeked through the logs at the men lying in the snow. They got General Montgomery, he said to himself. He knew the attack was over. He started to crawl away from the fence. As he moved, he left a thin line of blood behind him on the snow.

Benedict Arnold's men had smashed their way into the east end of Lower Town. Morgan led his men through the snowy, winding streets. Febiger led others toward the steep hill. The English were putting up a stiff fight. The Canadians were shooting from second-floor windows. The Americans were losing men.

Somehow Arnold led his men up the steep hill. There the street fighting went on. Then a musketball smashed into Arnold's leg. He fell. An officer told Dick and three other men to carry Arnold back into Lower Town.

The English began to win in Upper Town. Morgan and his men were captured. Febiger and his men had to give up. The Americans fell back. The English drove them down the hill and out of Lower Town.

The two beaten American armies met on the roads west of Quebec. Dick helped take Arnold to a farmhouse. There he found Will getting his arm fixed.

"We lost," said Dick, "we got beat near to death."

"We didn't even get into town," said Will. "They stopped us when they killed General Montgomery."

"Time to go home now. Time to go back to the farm," said Dick.

"Yep," said Will, "but what will we do the next time some colonel begins sweet-talking us?"

After Quebec

The Americans under Benedict Arnold
stayed in Canada that winter. Most of the men
who came with him went home. New troops
came up from Pennsylvania and Massachusetts.

In the spring, the English began to attack.
General Carleton drove the Americans west
along the St. Lawrence. He captured Montreal.
Then he drove south down the Richelieu River.
He won back Chambly and St. John.

In October, 1776, the two armies fought in
ships on Lake Champlain. Again the English
won. Colonel Arnold was now General Arnold,
but he couldn't win a battle. What he did win

was time. Because of him it was too late in the year for the English to attack New York.

Arnold and his few men fell back into Fort Ticonderoga. Carleton turned back. He wanted no part of a winter war on the rivers. He went back with his English soldiers to the Canadian towns on the St. Lawrence.

Over 5,000 Americans had died or been captured. They had failed to take Canada from the English. It was a low point of the war for the Americans.

Peace came to Ticonderoga. But the rivers and lakes would see war again in 1777. The English and Indians would come back. Ethan Allen had been right about that!

Epilogue

General Washington needed the cannons at Fort Ticonderoga. He sent Colonel Henry Knox to get them. Knox reached the fort on December 5, 1775. He picked 59 of the best cannons. They weighed 60 tons and Knox had to haul them 300 miles to Boston. With 42 strong sleds and 80 yoke of oxen, Knox's men pulled the cannons across frozen rivers, through forests, and over mountains. In late January, the cannons reached Washington's camp. With them, Washington was able to force the English to leave Boston in late March of 1776.

After Ethan Allen was captured, he was sent to England. He spent some time in the Pendennis Castle prison. For awhile, Allen thought he would be hanged as a rebel. In January, 1776, Allen and the other Americans were sent by ship to Halifax in Canada. After the English captured New York City, the prisoners were moved there. In May of 1778, Colonel Allen was exchanged for an English officer, Colonel Archibald Campbell. Allen went to Valley Forge and met General Washington. On the last day of May, Allen was back at Bennington with his Green Mountain Boys.

Benedict Arnold became a major general. He fought in other battles and was wounded again at Freeman's Farm. Arnold's second wife was a loyalist, and he began to make many loyalist friends. In August, 1780, Arnold was put in command of West Point, 50 miles up the Hudson from New York. What no American knew was that Arnold wanted to go over to the English side. He and General Clinton (at new York) had been writing secret letters. On September 23, 1780, the Americans picked up an Englishman by the name of John Anderson. Anderson turned out to be Major John Andre, one of Clinton's officers. In his shoes were papers and plans written by General Arnold. When Arnold heard Andre had been captured, he escaped. He was rowed down the Hudson to an English ship, the *Vulture*. Andre was hanged as a spy. Arnold was made a Brigadier General in the English army. He fought against the Americans, but won no important battles. Of all the American generals, Benedict Arnold was the only traitor.

IMPORTANT DATES OF THE REVOLUTION

1775	April 19	Fighting at Lexington and Concord
	May 10	Ethan Allen captures Fort Ticonderoga
	June 15	George Washington elected commander-in-chief of army
	June 16/17	Battle of Bunker (Breed's) Hill
	September	American soldiers invade Canada; Ethan Allen captured
	November/ December	British and Americans fight in Canada, South Carolina, New York, Virginia, Maine, and at sea
1776	March 17	British withdraw from Boston
	July 4	Congress adopts the Declaration of Independence
	August 27	Battle of Long Island; Americans retreat
	September 15	British take New York City
	September 16	Americans win Battle of Harlem Heights
	October 11/13	British fleet wins Battle of Lake Champlain
	October 28	British win at White Plains, N.Y.
	November 16	British take Fort Washington
	November 28	British take Rhode Island
	December	Washington takes army across Delaware and into Pennsylvania
	December 26	Washington wins Battle of Trenton, New Jersey

1777	January 3	Americans win Battle of Princeton
	January	American army winters at Morristown, New Jersey
	August 6	Battle of Oriskany, N. Y.
	August 16	Americans win Battle of Bennington, Vt.
	September 11	British win Battle of Brandywine
	September 26	British occupy Philadelphia
	October 4	British win Battle of Germantown
	October 6	British capture Forts Clinton and Montgomery
	October 7	Battles of Saratoga, N. Y.; British General Burgoyne's army surrenders October 17
	November 15	Articles of Confederation adopted
	December 18	Washington's army winters at Valley Forge
1778	February 6	France signs treaty of alliance with America
	June 18	British evacuate Philadelphia
	June 28	Americans win Battle of Monmouth Court House, N.J.
	July 4	George Rogers Clark wins at Kaskaskia
	August 29	Battle of Rhode Island; Americans retreat
	December 29	British capture Savannah, Ga.
1779	January	British take Vincennes, Ind.
	February 3	British lose at Charles Town, S.C.
	February 14	Americans win at Kettle Creek, Ga.
	February 20	Americans capture Vincennes
	March 3	British win at Briar Creek, Ga.
	June 20	Americans lose at Stono Ferry, S.C.
	July 16	Americans take Fort Stony Point, N. Y.
	August/ September	Fighting continues on land and sea. On September 23 John Paul Jones captures British *Serapis*
	December	Americans winter at Morristown, N.J.
1780	May 12	Charles Town surrenders to British
	June 20	Battle of Ramsour's Mills, N. C.
	July 30	Battle of Rocky Mount, S. C.
	September 26	Battle of Charlotte, N. C.
	October 7	Battle of King's Mountain, S. C.
1781	January 17	Americans win Battle of Cowpens, S. C.
	March/April	Battles in North Carolina, South Carolina, Virginia, Georgia
	October 19	British army surrenders at Yorktown
1782	July 11	British leave Savannah, Ga.
	November 30	Preliminary peace signed between America and Britain
	December 14	British leave Charleston, S. C.
1783	September 3	Final peace treaty signed
	November 25	British evacuate New York City

About the Authors:

Susan Dye Lee has been writing professionally since she graduated from college in 1961. Working with the Social Studies Curriculum Center at Northwestern University, she has created course materials in American studies. Ms. Lee has also co-authored a text on Latin America and Canada, written case studies in legal history for the Law in American Society Project, and developed a teacher's guide for tapes that explore women's role in America's past. The writer credits her students for many of her ideas. Currently, she is doing research for her history dissertation on the Women's Christian Temperance Union for Northwestern University. In her free moments, Susan Lee enjoys traveling, playing the piano, and welcoming friends to "Highland Cove," the summer cottage she and her husband, John, share.

John R. Lee enjoys a prolific career as a writer, teacher, and outdoorsman. After receiving his doctorate in social studies at Stanford, Dr. Lee came to Northwestern University's School of Education, where he advises student teachers and directs graduates in training. A versatile writer, Dr. Lee has co-authored the Scott-Foresman social studies textbooks for primary-age children. In addition, he has worked on the production of 50 films and over 100 filmstrips. His biographical film on Helen Keller received a 1970 Venice Film Festival award. His college text, *Teaching Social Studies in the Elementary School*, has recently been published. Besides pro-football, Dr. Lee's passion is his Wisconsin cottage, where he likes to shingle leaky roofs, split wood, and go sailing.

About the Artist:

Robert Ulm, a Chicago resident, has been an advertising and editorial artist in both New York and Chicago. Mr. Ulm is a successful painter as well as an illustrator. In his spare time he enjoys fishing and playing tennis.